# T-Rump the T-Rex

By R. A. Combs

In the horrible past, not so long, long ago,

In the gauche, gaudy ballrooms of Mara-La-Go,

A T-Rex named T-Rump lived, happy and vile,

Secure in his role as an alpha reptile.

"I'm such a success!" he opined to himself.

"I have to make sure to tell everyone else

Of the glorious tale of the greatness of ME!

I'll show them the winner that they'll never be!"

He opened his windows, he bellowed his name,

He called for attention … but nobody came.

"What's this?" he complained,

"Do they not give a damn?

Is no one aware of how awesome I am?

If I can't improve all their plain little lives

With news of my ventures, my exploits, my wives,

Then life's not worth living, for them or for ME!

They have to live my life vicariously!"

He trudged to his TV, upset and confused,

And — after a struggle — he turned on the news.

(The problem, most likely, arose from demands

That remote controls make on such miniscule hands.)

And T-Rump, well, he didn't like what he saw.

Reasoned discussions! Respect for the law!

A nationwide trend toward inclusion and order

And making things better both sides of the border.

The T-Rex kept looking at all this humanity,

Seeing it all as a threat to his vanity.

"Where is the ugliness? Where's the insanity?"

(Guess he forgot to switch over to Hannity.)

"None of this goodness does ME any good,

Or helps ME obtain all the fame that I should.

With everyone acting so sane and progressive,

There's no one to care that I'm just this impressive.

I don't like this system!

This system must stop!

And I know where the blame should go:

Straight to the top!"

And then, an idea plopped into his brain.

"Our leader is failing; this land's down the drain.

I'm the best thing about it, that's easy to see.

What's wrong with this land is there's not enough ME!"

The moment he thought it, he knew he must act.

With typical hustle and absence of tact,

He forged a great plan to bring T-Rump to all:

A plan for a beautiful, terrible wall.

A wall long enough to stretch clear 'cross the land,

From the big city streets to the dry desert sand,

From the wide ocean shores to the white mountain snow,

To the vulgar verandas of Mara-La-Go.

"And the best thing," said T-Rump, "is not just the size.

It's how I'll construct it and how it's comprised:

A wall made of people! A people-filled wall!

With ME, mighty leader, on top of it all!"

And at that very moment, on that very day,

His head swelled ten sizes beneath his toupee.

"So, why not a tower?" he heard

from behind.

He turned around quickly,

despairing to find

That his wife had been hovering,

listening in.

"Your towers are great!" she said through a forced grin.

"You make so much money with all those locations.

Why, all of your towers just scream 'compensation'!

Imagine the income a tower could bring

That is made out of people with you as their king!"

"It's not for the money!" her husband replied,

"I do this for vanity, ego, and pride!

Far nobler reasons! In fact, I intend

To do this, no matter how much I must spend!

Besides," he went on (as his wife's interest waned),

"A tower's no good for this plan in my brain.

A tower of people just might be brought low

By some malcontent griping alone far below.

But a wall," he continued, "is just what I need

To control every person I hanker to lead.

There's no better way to keep people in line

And make sure that their heads never rise above mine."

And with that, he ran straight out of Mara-La-Go

And arrived in the heartland and started the show.

"You hicks and you hayseeds have suffered too long

Without ME to save you. You're doing it wrong!

You know, well as I do, our leader's a fraud,

He has to be foreign! His looks are, well, odd!

You say that you've had it. You march, and you speak,

But the party you're throwing is worthless and weak!

Your tea is just sad! But I know how you like it.

You'll party with ME if you just let ME spike it!"

Apparently, some people liked what they heard,

And followed him, hanging on word after word.

And oh, there were plenty of words to go 'round!

For T-Rump loved nothing so much as the sound

Of his lizardlike voice seething out to the masses,

Filling their heads and igniting their asses.

"Come near, and discover your hero of heroes!

I started with nothing! Well, just a few zeroes!

And now, I'm a titan! An icon! A brand!

Isn't that what you need from the boss of this land?"

He spoke of his conquests, admitted no faults,

(He left out his bankruptcies, breakups, assaults … ),

And the louder he bellowed, the more people came,

To cheer at his boasts and to shout out his name.

They let him point fingers. They let him play God.

And they dumped all their tea just to harbor a fraud.

"Get in line!" T-Rump shouted. "One line for you all!

You're now the foundation of my giant wall!"

They followed along and stood shoulder to shoulder,

And huddled for warmth in a world suddenly colder.

He gave them each caps, all the same color red,

To protect from his claws as he marched on their heads.

He scrambled atop, took a brief look around,

And he said, "Now this wall has to cover more ground.

Those moralist fruitcakes, they sure need a winner,

But they prefer saints, and I'm such a sinner!"

But that didn't stop him or make him play fairer.

"If I can't be holy, I'll wage holy terror!"

"Hello evangelicals! I stand for piety!

Also, intolerance! Dread! And anxiety!

Pray all you want, while I prey on your fears:

Without ME in charge, our whole world disappears!

I know that you'll join ME. Just call it a hunch!

Never mind that I broke four commandments since lunch!"

And the T-Rex was right, for those proud bible-thumpers

Anointed that mammon-gorged camera-humper.

And as they lined up to be part of his wall,

He looked all around and he said, "Still too small.

To rule everybody — just based on my math —

I'll need to fool more of 'em … closer to half!"

And so he picked targets, and set his priorities:

No wasting time courting women, minorities,

People of other faiths, people with brains,

People with acronyms after their names,

People in cities, or on either shore,

People once foreign but aren't anymore,

People who stoop to help those on their knees,

People who stand on behalf of the trees,

People who care for the fate of the earth,

People who look beyond places of birth,

And people who never have said to themselves,

"It's me against them, and screw everyone else."

He knew they'd reject him if he ever tried.

"They're jealous of all of my greatness!" he lied.

But then, there were others so eager, he knew,

To answer his call, just a whistle would do.

And sure enough, just the right note, here and there —

Delivered by birds sent off tweeting in air —

Ushered deplorables in by the basket,

A bloc that would do any task he would ask it.

Bigots, and bullies, and birthers, and trolls,

Supremacist types who prefer hoods with holes,

Misogynists, militants, anarchists too,

They heard every whistle he wanted them to.

And in they came, barking and woofing and panting.

He lined them alt right up beneath him, while chanting, "It's time that your voices were finally heard! I'll speak for you all, 'cause I have the best words!"

And yet, his new wall was still lacking in size.

"It's time," T-Rump said, "to pursue the big prize.

I'll fight the establishment, trash their elites,

And send every frontrunner down to defeat!

The kingmakers think I'm the lowest of low

And that I'll never stop them from running the show.

But I'll go lower still! I know just where I'll nab 'em!

Like women, 'twill be by the Bush that I'll grab 'em!

From there, I'll start mowing my way through the pack:

They'll play by the rules while I play to attack!

Eviscerate! Insult! Emasculate too!

Do all of the things that no leader should do!"

And as each competitor fell to his plans,

He knew just the way to appeal to their fans.

"Your party's behemoths, they trumpet and stomp,

And state their respect for tradition and pomp.

They say that I'm dangerous, say that I'm crass,

And say you can't follow a king without class.

Well they're history. I'm economics! You choose:

My class makes you richer and theirs makes you lose.

Good luck hanging on to your idols of old;

Just idolize ME, 'cause I'm made of pure gold!

And once I'm in charge, I will turn this whole scene

Into one classless, gigantic money machine!"

And he thundered his way through the big party tent,

And the things that he said, and the message he sent,

And the money he spent,

And the truth that he bent,

Kept those pachyderms loyal, 100 percent.

They donned their red ballcaps. The great wall extended.

The T-Rex beamed out — then his confidence ended.

The wall was so long, but not quite long enough,

And he knew there was nobody else he could bluff.

"I don't like this system! This system is rigged!"

He threatened to boycott, but then — he reneged.

For then, out of nowhere, some strange things occurred.

It's hard to explain, or to put into words.

There were fakers, and leakers, and Wieners anew,

Commies, and Comeys, and Colleges too.

And most of all, people who couldn't be bothered

To vote for a figure that's not like their father's.

And when the dust settled, and as the smoke rose

(It still doesn't sound right to say, but here goes),

T-Rump was triumphant! Somehow he prevailed,

And his wall made of people, which previously failed

To extend even halfway across the great land

Now drew everybody beneath his command.

Yes, those who resisted him, those who stood tall,

Were now forced to stand as just part of his wall —

To weather his hatred, abide by his laws,

And, capless, withstand the full weight of his claws.

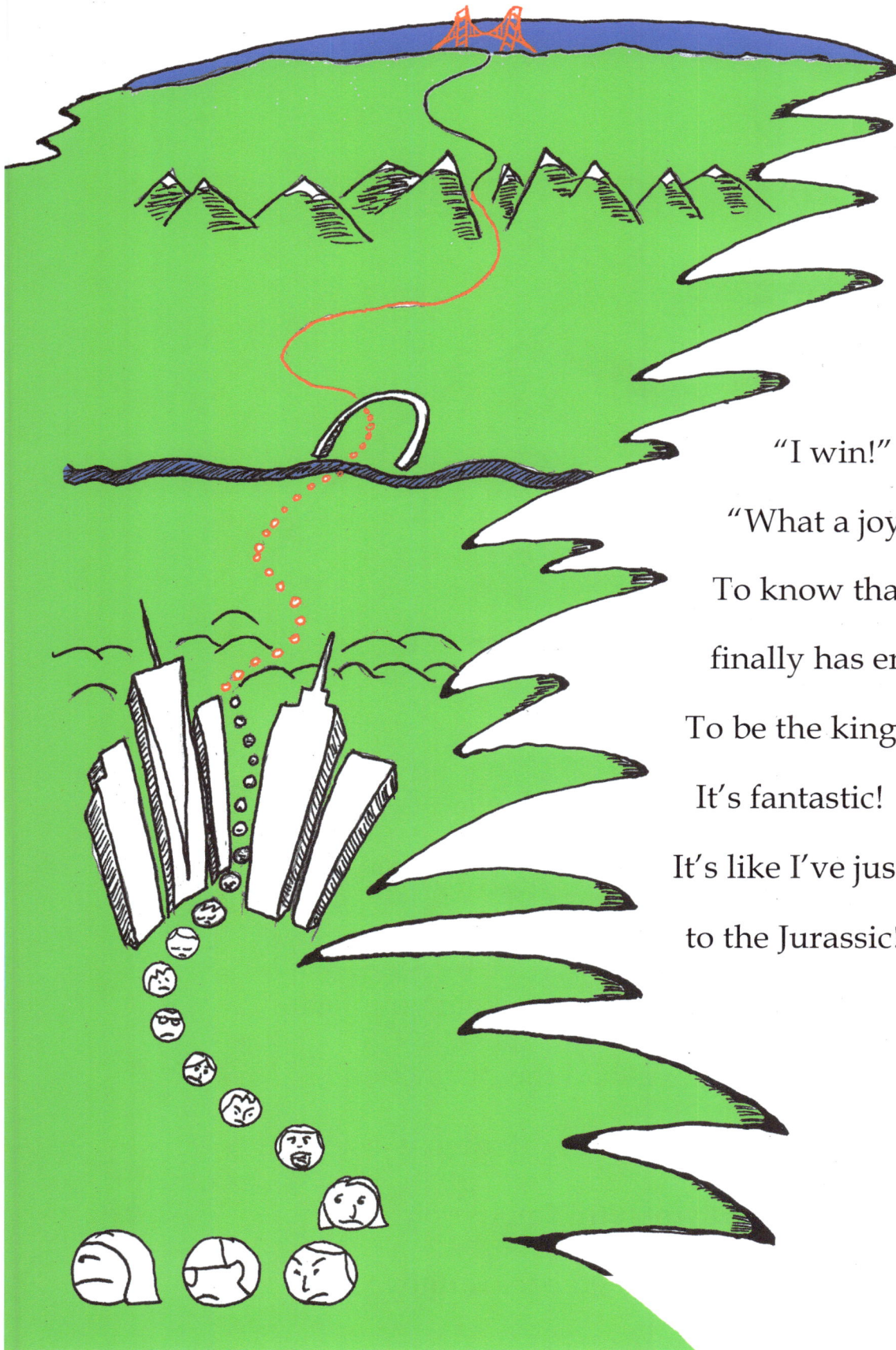

"I win!" he enthused.

"What a joy it must be,

To know that this land

finally has enough ME!

To be the king T-Rex is huge!

It's fantastic!

It's like I've just sent us back

to the Jurassic!"

And then, from somewhere in the wall, far behind,

He heard a small voice rising up from the line.

"Excuse me," it said, "Not to spoil your big scene,

"But I think the Cretaceous is more what you mean.

It was then that the T-Rexes had the distinction

Of ruling the world — Of course, 'til their extinction.

You see, it all changed when this meteoroid …"

"Silence!" the T-Rex king yelled back, annoyed.

"That climate change nonsense means nothing to ME!

You think that I care about science? You'll see!"

And he turned, with intention to retaliate,

With his usual mix of hyperbole and hate,

But all that he saw was a long line of red,

So he couldn't be sure of who said what they said.

"Humph," he said, shrugging. "Well, I'm not concerned.

Where was I? Oh yes. What a victory I earned!

It's over," he crowed, "but it's just the beginning!

I hope you all never get tired of winning!

'Cause now that, at last, this land has enough ME,

I'll be the great leader I promised I'd be!"

And he rolled up his sleeves,

And embarked on his mission,

And fucked it all up beyond all recognition.

He chose for his helpers some folks that he shouldn't.

He tried to pass laws before finding he couldn't.

He said he was wise but then showed that he isn't.

He shielded some cronies who should be imprisoned.

He schmoozed with his daughter, he oozed inexperience,

Confused Irish poets with rhyming Nigerians,

Blocked every move to curb rich wheeler-dealers,

Defended white marchers, degraded black kneelers,

Handed down orders based mainly on grudges,

Bullied reporters, employees, and judges,

Sent his own ships the wrong way by mistake,

And bombed foreign lands over chocolate cake.

He hired on a whim and he fired on a lark

And let islanders fend for themselves in the dark.

Junkets were furnished, and gold stars were tarnished,

Ignorance burnished, duplicity varnished,

Insults were brandished, and chaos was relished,

And IQs and crowd sizes grossly embellished.

And as he moved on from one fail to the next,

He heard, down below, a voice sounding perplexed.

"You told us you knew what you're doing," it said.

"But it looks like you're making this up in your head.

You're acting confused and unhinged. Are you well?

From down here below, it's not easy to tell.

Perhaps you could do with a good diagnosis.

This could be the sign of some kind of psychosis."

"You!" roared the T-Rex. "I told you to shush!

So now you're an expert on health? Not so much!"

He still couldn't see whose voice rose from the wall,

So he bellowed and boasted and bragged to them all.

"I'm the expert on health! Believe ME, it's easy!

My biggest win yet (and perhaps my most sleazy)

Will be to free all of you, free as a bird,

From the cage you've been stuck in, so safely insured.

It's time that you people cared less about health

And more 'bout aspiring to privilege and wealth!

That's the best medicine! That's my Rx!

Get rich, then get healthy!" prescribed the T-Rex.

"So I'll fix this whole system. It's low-hanging fruit,

But I'd rather just rip it all up by the root.

And if someone fights ME? I'll win and they'll lose!

I'll make them an offer no one could refuse!"

And he pandered, then threatened, then gave ultimatums,

And managed to make even right-wingers hate him.

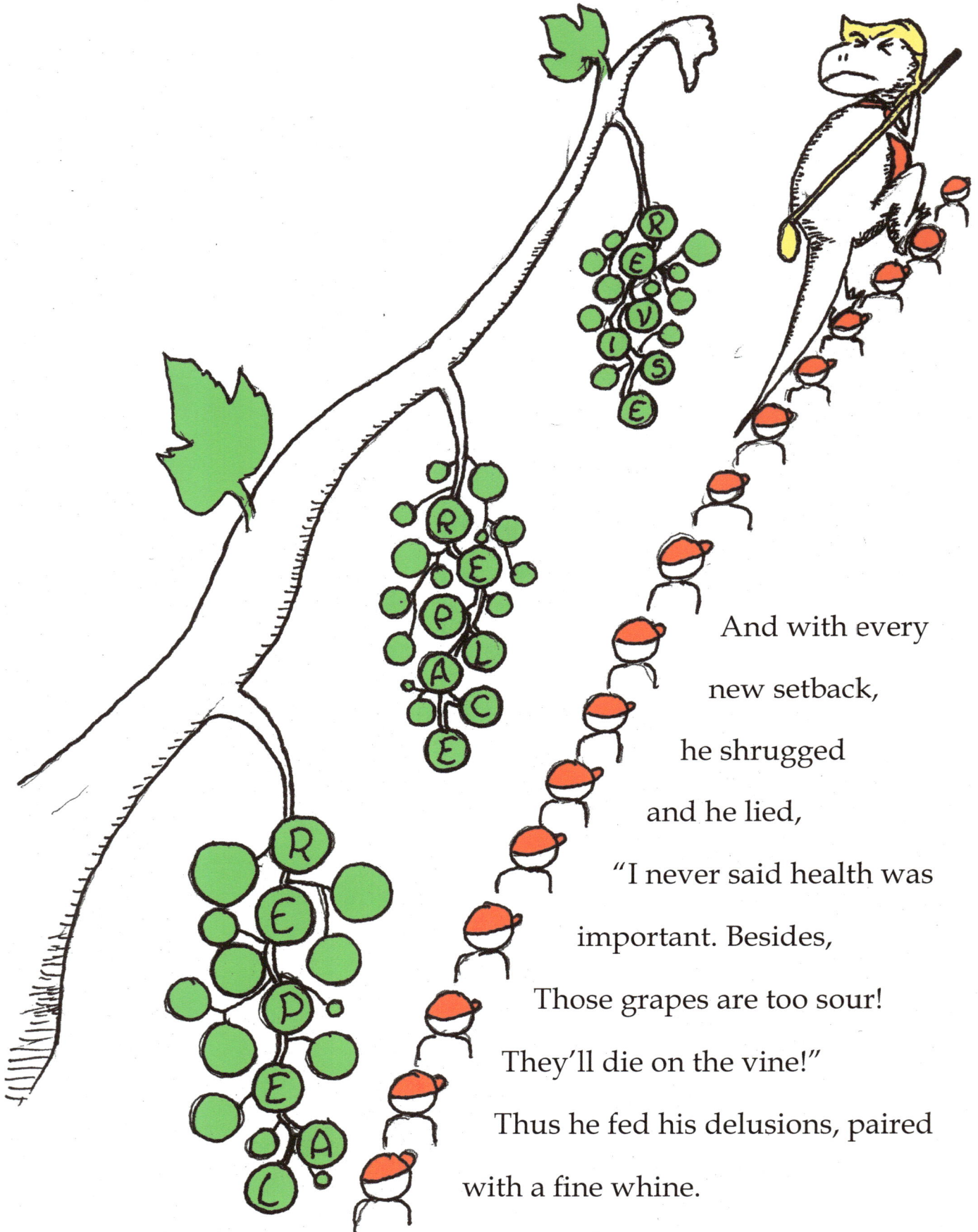

And with every

new setback,

he shrugged

and he lied,

"I never said health was

important. Besides,

Those grapes are too sour!

They'll die on the vine!"

Thus he fed his delusions, paired

with a fine whine.

"Wait a minute!" a voice said.

"What happened to winning?

That's all you've been talking of since the beginning."

"Whoever you are, I have had it with you!"

The T-Rex lashed out. "I'll destroy you! I'll sue!

You want to see winning? This wall is my win!

I've built it myself with you losers within!

And I dance on your heads, and I'm fueled by one thought:

That this land needs more ME,

And I'm ME,

And you're not!

Why don't you be helpful, instead of belligerent?

This is a wall! Stand your ground and be vigilant!

The same goes for all of you! Enemies lurk!

They're coming to get you! Look sharp! Get to work!"

The people obeyed, and looked out from the wall

At the multitudes bent on destroying them all,

And here's what they saw: people trying to live

In times that demanded more than they could give.

From all 'round the world, some with families, some lone,

They hungered to salvage some semblance of home.

Or they came for the promise of chances anew,

To do all the work that few natives would do.

Or they already lived here, secure all along,

And found themselves outside but did nothing wrong.

Whatever the reason, whatever the dream,

They didn't fit into his monstrous scheme.

"You see?" T-Rump yelled.

"They're bad hombres! Fanaticals!

Different! Darker! And totally radical!

They'll never fit in, so let's keep them all out.

After all, isn't that what a wall is about?"

"I don't know,"

Came a voice from somewhere down below,

"They're mostly just normal. Why make them all go?

Perhaps we can tweak this, and go with what works?

And leave out the part where we're paranoid jerks?

I know there are options. I read in the news … "

But the lizard king's face assumed violent new hues.

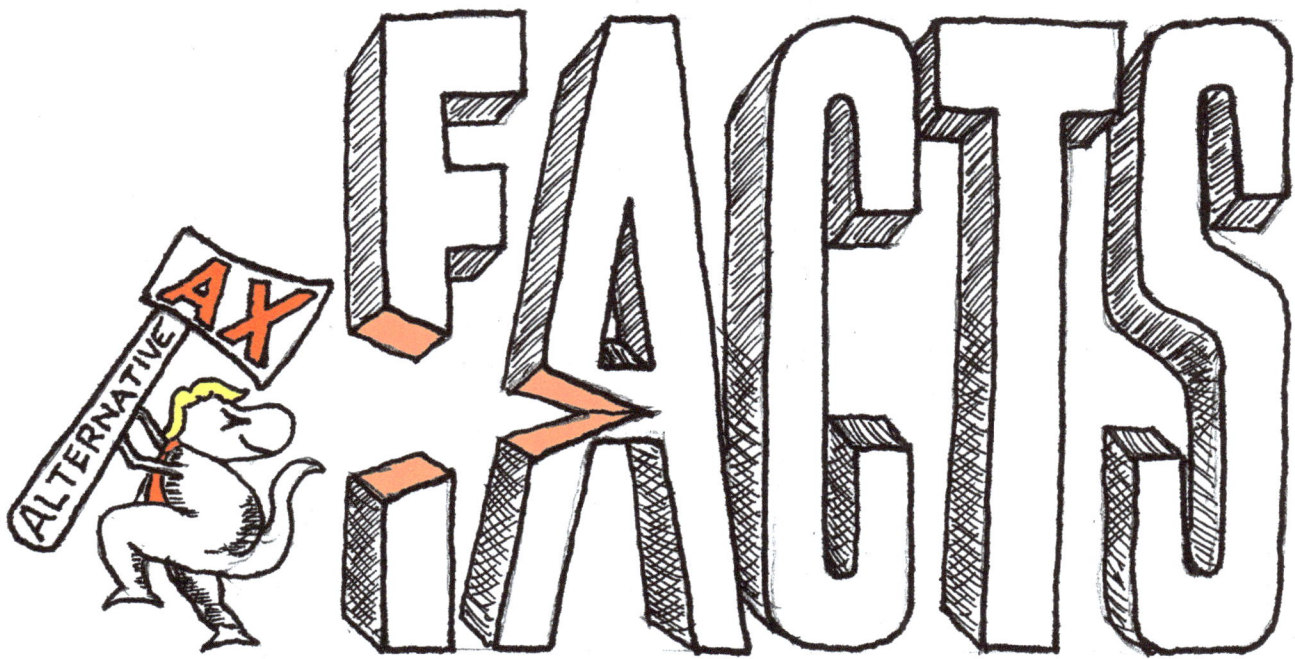

"The news!" he thought, cringing. "Those muckracking hacks!

It's an ax that they're grinding — an ax made of facts!

I'll never allow it. I'll take my own whacks!

I'll whack those hacks with my alternative ax!"

He yelled down below, "Now don't be so naïve!

The press can't be trusted, believe ME! Believe!

They've been very nasty to ME, so unfair,

By putting the words that I say on the air,

And having the gall to report what I do,

And daring to show how it all affects you.

They just want to get my big nose out of joint,

So don't hear what they say

And don't look where they point!"

"In fact, turn around!" T-Rump suddenly thundered.

"There's nothing out there, just in case you all wondered.

There's nothing out there that I want you to see,

I'll clean it up later, so leave it to ME!

Instead, turn around, and don't burden your eyes

With those terrorist schemes and those media lies!"

So the people obeyed and, as one, turned around,

And they looked,

And they couldn't believe what they found.

Sprawled out before them, in one giant scene,

A country club stretched, artificially green.

"Now this," T-Rump boasted,

"Is something worth seeing!

It's my secret world! Look how secret I'm being!

It's under construction, but I can't resist.

I have to show off or I'll cease to exist!

It's big-league tremendous! So classy! So nice!

Go on, feast your eyes upon my paradise!"

And as they all looked, not too sure what to think,

They saw people gathering there on the links.

Cronies, conspirators, cads with their caddies,

Little-time hustlers and world-class baddies

Were all making deals while they played a few rounds

On the huge private course on the country club grounds.

There were bankers who frolicked where sandtraps once lay,

For the crews removed hazards the very first day.

(They did a good job with their care and maintaining,

Except for a swamp no one got 'round to draining.)

And then there were arms dealers, oil moguls too,

Unhindered by course rules and all playing through.

There were press secretaries improving their lies,

Accountants whose scorecards went unscrutinized,

Cabinet members who smashed their own clubs,

Philanderers wearing their putters to nubs,

Budgeteers slicing and lobbyists hooking,

Generals cringing when no one was looking,

And elephants testing the wind from the rough,

Trying to tell when enough was enough.

Nutjobs and blowhards caroused in the fringe

And spouted their drivel unfettered, unhinged.

And all throughout, running, a rabid Fox chattered,

Reminding the players of who really mattered.

But the loudest, most boisterous group on the course

Was led by a shirtless bald czar on a horse,

Who fostered the country club since the beginning,

Yet cared not for golfing but only for winning.

So, there they all reveled, a club all their own,

With skin colors ranging from ecru to bone.

And everywhere, any place it could be stuck,

Was the big name of T-Rump, high muckety-muck.

"It's perfect. It's beautiful!" sighed the T-Rex,

"And now you are witness to all this success!

Just look at who came! Just take in the view!

Oh, the biggest of names! A who's who of not you!

My world just gets better! My influence broader!

My son-in-law cooler! My daughter much hotter!"

But then, the bald horseman called out from the grounds:

"Yo, comrade! What gives? Turn those people around!

The things going on in here, nobody sees.

There's business to do, so some privacy please!"

The T-Rex frowned. "Privacy? I'm fine without it.

What good is this job if I can't brag about it?

But fine. Tell my people to keep things discreet,

At least till I blow it all up with a tweet!"

"But this is disgusting!" a voice below cried.

"You said you were one of us. Look how you've lied!

Behind the great wall, and our backs the whole time,

Is this den of corruption and excess and crime.

Is this what we asked for? Is this why we voted?

For you to be pampered? Your toadies promoted?"

The T-Rex just shrugged. "Don't appreciate beauty?

Well you're not important, so just do your duty!

You don't enjoy winning? Don't like what you see?

That's fine, all you need is to look up to ME!"

"Look up, and remember

the reason I won!

It's because

I'm the greatest,

the A-number-one!

And you know

what? If you're still

not liking the view,

There's millions of us

and there's just one of you!

You gripe all alone, so if you can't abide,

Then do ME a favor and just step aside!

Now tell ME, you malcontent, tell ME you see

That everything's great in a land with more ME!"

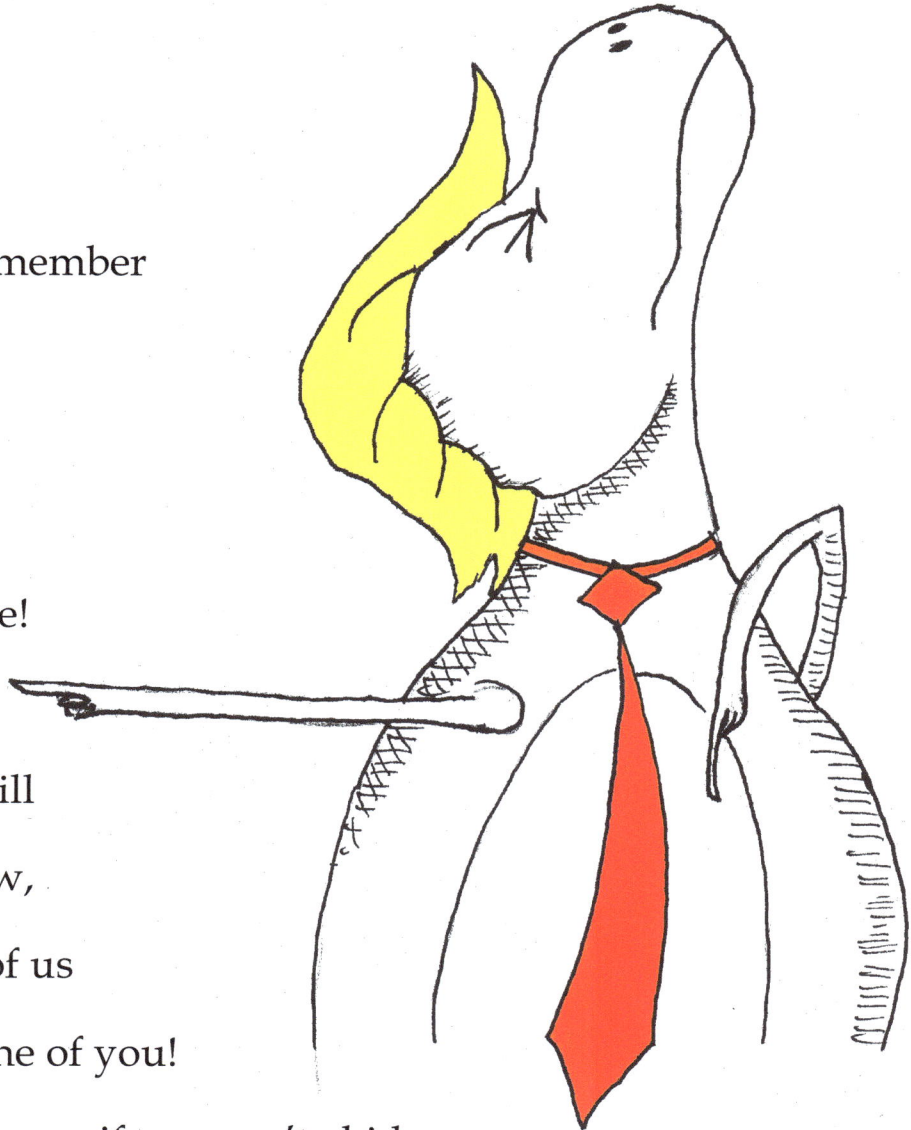

And every cap lifted, and every head cocked,

And every eye fixed on the beast as he talked.

"You know," said a voice in a confident tone.

"You have a good point. I should go it alone."

"But here is the thing," said another voice, clear,

"You certainly talk better than you can hear."

A third asked, "Did you really think all along

That you're arguing just with one person? You're wrong!"

Another chimed in, "We all have different voices.

We set our own paths and we make our own choices."

"To you, we've been just one annoyance, so small.

But you packed a whole bunch of us into your wall."

"You really know nothing of us down below you,

But we've had the chance now of getting to know you."

"And now you command that we look at you. Fine.

So here's what we see from our places in line."

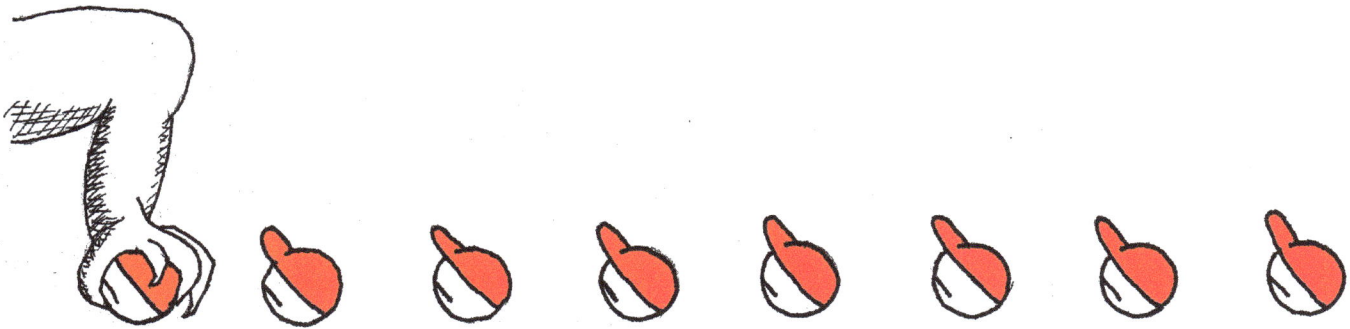

"A childish pretender in over his head."

"A snake-oil shill who sells favors instead."

"A dealmaker dealing in hatred and dread."

"A thin-skinned alarmist who always sees red."

"A loose-cannon hothead who'd leave us all dead."

"An orange cartoon clown with a Chia-Pet head."

"A racist." "A narcissist."

"Hypocrite." "Fraud."

"A liar." "An imbecile."

"Self-styled god."

"But most of all, what we can see, most distinct,

Is a dinosaur, rapidly going extinct.

We can't wait around for a meteoroid —

Not with all you've dismantled and all you've destroyed.

Let's give you your wish. Everyone, one and all,

Who's had it with T-Rump, step out from the wall!"

And the T-Rex looked down and with shock on his face,

He saw his wall shifting all over the place.

At one end, the capless ones gleefully scatted,

While he looked more fearfully toward the red-hatted.

And soon, those caps started to fly through the air,

As people stepped out of the line everywhere.

Beneath him, extruding themselves from his talons,

Some bolted and left him there, losing his balance.

With a shriek, the old lizard galumphed cap to cap,

Then ran, best he could, dodging gap after gap.

"It can't be!" he hollered, "This land needs more ME!"

Then onto that land he was dumped, harmlessly.

And the people who caused him to fall with a splat,

Took off on their own, heading this way and that.

Some helped the outsiders. Some joined with the press.

Some cleaned up the country club, clearing the mess.

Most returned to their lives, but vowed to be smarter

And make things for demagogue dinosaurs harder.

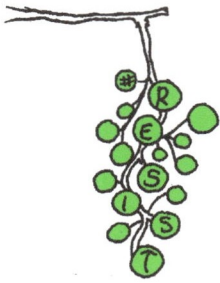

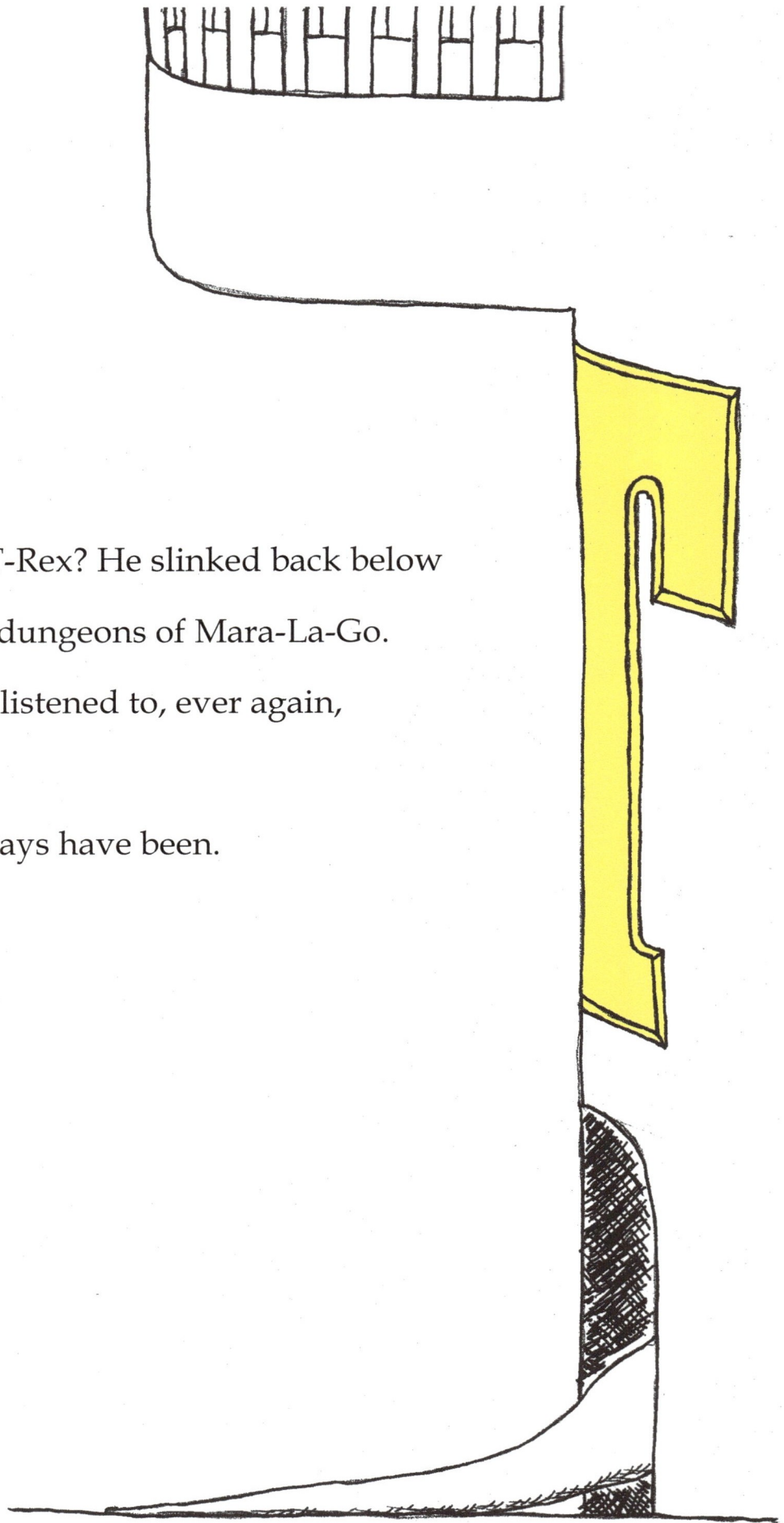

And T-Rump the T-Rex? He slinked back below

To the dim, dingy dungeons of Mara-La-Go.

And he never was listened to, ever again,

Just like, maybe,

How it should always have been.


THE END

www.ingramcontent.com/pod-product-compliance
Lightning Source LLC
Chambersburg PA
CBHW060814090426
42737CB00002B/60